ALL THINGS RABBITS FOR KIDS

FILLED WITH PLENTY OF FACTS, PHOTOS, AND FUN TO LEARN ALL ABOUT BUNNIES

ANIMAL READS

THIS BOOK BELONGS TO...

____

____

WWW.ANIMALREADS.COM

CONTENTS

AN INTRODUCTION TO RABBITS

Of all the animals in the world, there is no doubt that rabbits are among the most beloved. *Because what's not to love?*

Rabbits are downright adorable, with their fluffy bums, furry ears, and button noses. So adorable, in fact, that they have been featured in children's stories, films, and cartoons since ***fur***ever: from the mystical Easter Bunny to the mischievous Bugs Bunny and Disney's very own Roger Rabbit.

If you love rabbits just as much (if not more!) as we do, then we know you will want to know all about them, right?

Want to discover where rabbits absolutely *love* to live, what they eat, how they have evolved through time, and how to care for them the right way?

Then what are you waiting for?

Hippity-hoppity on board, and let's get to know them better!

WHAT'S INVISIBLE AND SMELLS LIKE CARROTS?

Rabbit Farts!

WHAT IS A RABBIT?

Rabbits belong to the animal family called **Leporidae**, which includes rabbits and hares. You probably think that rabbits and hares are pretty much the same animal because they look so alike, but if you did, you'd be *hopping* to the wrong conclusion.

In reality, rabbits and hares are different animal species that belong to the same family. Much like dogs and foxes belong to the same animal family (the Canidae) but are different species. So, it would be wise to consider rabbits and hares as distant cousins rather than siblings.

The most important difference between rabbits and hares is in their personality. While rabbits are mostly calm, friendly, and even cuddly, hares can be skittish and love their independence.

This is why rabbits have been what is called, **domesticated** (which means they have learned to live side by side with humans), but hares prefer to live in the wild.

Anywho… where were we?

Oh yes…RABBITS!

There are about **50 different breeds of rabbits** in the world, which is probably more than you ever imagined. But the rabbit is one of the most **adaptable** animals in the world, which means it can live in all sorts of places, no matter how cold, hot, dry, or wet.

In fact, rabbits live in *almost* every country, and their ability to make themselves at home anywhere (to adapt!) has meant their total numbers on earth are staggering.

Today, researchers believe there are about 710 million rabbits alive in the world!

Now *THAT'S* crazy!

Rabbits are usually small to medium-sized animals that grow to about the size of a standard cat. Some giant breeds, however, can grow to the size of dogs! Later on, we will meet a few of the most interesting breeds of rabbits, so make sure to keep reading!

Rabbits are **mammals**, which means they have fur (*d'uh!*) and give birth to live babies, called kittens (*yes, just like cat babies!*), which feed on their mother's milk. If you are now thinking that rabbits, cats, dogs, and humans have a few things in common... **you'd be right!**

We are ALL mammals too!

FUN FACT: Almost all mammals give birth to live young and don't lay eggs. But, did you know that there are a few mammals that actually lay eggs? Yes, as a matter of fact, there are two! The echidna and the duck-billed platypus!

The single best-known fact about rabbits is that they **reproduce fast**, which means they can have a lot of babies in a very short period of time.

Want to know an interesting story?

Wild rabbits were first introduced in Australia in 1859 (that's 160 years ago!) The original group was made up of only 24 rabbits. This group reproduced soooo quickly that, just six years later, the colony of rabbits numbered 200,000!

Now that we've got to know rabbits better, let's talk about some of the most popular species!

WHAT DO YOU CALL A HAPPY RABBIT?

A hop-timist!

DIFFERENT RABBIT SPECIES

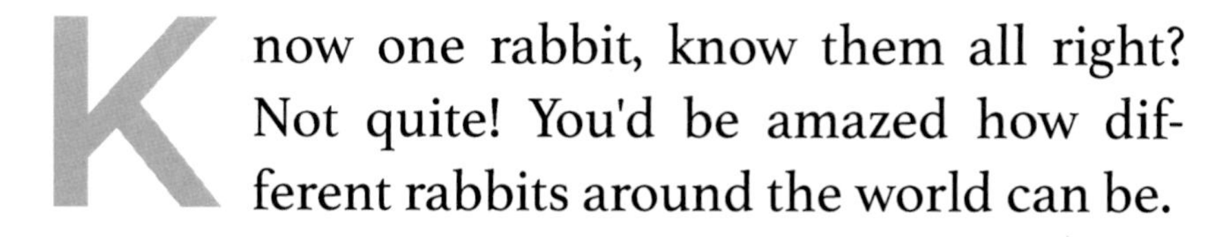

Know one rabbit, know them all right? Not quite! You'd be amazed how different rabbits around the world can be.

Now let's go ahead and meet some of the best known and most interesting rabbit species of all.

AMERICAN RABBIT

The American Rabbit is one of the most recognizable rabbit breeds in the world, considered the '*classic*' rabbit with snow-white fur and a very sweet personality. What's interesting about the American Rabbit is that it actually came from Europe, originally.

The American Rabbit became an official breed back in 1917. What many people also don't know is that the original American Rabbits was actually blue/grey, with no white spots at all. Then breeders began mating these blue rabbits with **rare albino white rabbits** – these were rabbits that missed out on color altogether, so their skin and eyes are pink, and their fur is white. This mix-n-match created the classic white American Rabbit we know today.

Originally, this rabbit breed was named the German Blue Vienna Rabbit, but because there was a BIG war between Germany and America (called World War I), the name was changed to American Rabbit.

American Rabbits were heavily bred and farmed for their fur and meat in the US for many years. Then came new breeds that had even better fur and meat for humans to use, so this breed was pretty much ignored. As a result, the breed became endangered, which means their numbers were going down very quickly.

Luckily, conservation projects started about 20 years ago to help protect this very special animal. In the last 10 years, the popularity of the American Rabbit has been increasing, so their numbers are now on the rise.

The American Rabbit weighs about 12 pounds, with the females being slightly bigger than the males. This rabbit has a half-arched body shape and is considered among the largest of the 'normal sized' rabbits. They can also live up to around 12 years of age.

FUN FACT: Rabbits are found on all continents, except Antarctica!

FLEMISH GIANT RABBIT

As you may have guessed, the Flemish Giant is indeed positively huge. This is the largest rabbit breed in the world and also one of the oldest.

The Flemish Giant Rabbit Federation was originally founded in 1915, making this perhaps the oldest known registered rabbit breed in the US.

The Flemish can weigh a whopping 20 pounds when fully grown and measure an amazing 2.5 feet in length. They can be found in seven distinct colors and are known to make excellent pets.

Originally, and as was the case with all domesticated rabbits, the Giant Flemish was bred specifically for its fur and meat. However, they soon proved to have a very gentle personality, so people began to keep them as pets instead. *Now wasn't that a great decision?*

As will all domesticated rabbits, the Flemish is sweet and docile, but it's important to know that all rabbits can bite if handled roughly.

FUN FACT: This breed originated in the northern region of Belgium called Flanders in the 16th century. There, the official language is Flemish, which is where this breed got its name! Most historians agree that sailors brought Giant Flemish rabbits to the United States around 1890.

PYGMY RABBIT

Now that we know all about the world's largest rabbit breed, let's talk about the smallest. *Say hello to the Pygmy Rabbit.*

The Pygmy Rabbit is as cute as they come. This breed is **native** to the United States, which means it was not brought here from other continents by humans like the Flemish Giant was. It is also the only native US species of rabbits that dig their own burrows. The Pygmy rabbits are not only the smallest of all rabbits but the smallest of all *leporids*.

They are gray in color, have short ears and hind legs, and do not have any white fuzzy fur at all. The Pygmy only weighs around 1 pound (***that's TINY!***) and measures around 11 inches in length. Found mainly along the north-western side of the US, the Pygmy Rabbit survives on sagebrush wilderness. A wide-open space covered in the thick sagebrush, which the Pygmy eats for food and uses for shelter.

The sagebrush is a very important ecosystem in the United States, and it supports a wide range of animals, including deer, elk, pronghorn (a type of antelope!), many different birds, and of course, wild pygmy rabbits!

IMPORTANT FACT: The Pygmy looks like it might make a great pet because it's so tiny (and cute!), but in reality, this is one of the wildest rabbit breeds in the world. It has never been domesticated and prefers to live out its life in the beautiful sagebrush wilderness. If you ever see one in the wild, remember to just admire it from a distance, and take photos if you can. As with all wild animals, always keep a safe distance!

LOP EARED RABBITS

Often described as puffs of fluff, lop-eared rabbits are a whole line of rabbits that are distinctive because their ears do not stand up like, say, American Rabbits, but hang down kinda floppily to either side of their round heads. On larger breeds, the floppy ears can hang down to the ground!

Right now, there are about 15 different breeds of lop-eared rabbits. They include the sweet Holland Lop (one of the smallest), the Mini Lop (actually bigger than the Holland!), and the French Lop, perhaps the most popular lop rabbit in the United States and the largest, coming in at about 10 pounds!

Every lop rabbit has a unique set of characteristics, which means they come in all sorts of shapes, sizes, colors, and also personalities. They all have one thing in common, however, and that's their floppy ears!

FUN FACT: The French Lop is the most common breed of domesticated rabbits in the US. It is large, sociable, and sweet, although – as with all lop rabbits – needs very special care. Long floppy ears can easily pick up dirt from the ground, which, if not cleaned out, can cause ear infections. Ouch! Their large size also means they need plenty of outdoor space for exercise.

BLANC DE HOTOT

Another very distinct rabbit is the Blanc de Hotot, and in case you can't tell from its fancy name, it originated from France. Fancy in name and looks, the Blanc de Hotot sports eye makeup! Or, at least, that's what it looks like! Their big round eyes are lines with a dark stripe, making them look very glamorous indeed. Coupled with a fluffy white fur, this rabbit certainly looks like a Hollywood superstar.

Although they were treated like pet celebrities many years ago, their popularity decreased over the last few decades. The Blanc, nowadays, is considered **endangered**, meaning there aren't too many left in the world. Part of the reason is that although they are somewhat friendly, the Blanc de Hotot is a bit of a loner and prefers to be left alone.

DUTCH

The Dutch Rabbit, more commonly known as just Dutch, is one of the most recognizable species of rabbits, specifically for its unique markings.

They have a black and white body. With a white face and black eyes and ears. It really looks like they're all dressed up for a masquerade ball!

Once upon a time, this was the most popular pet breed of rabbits in the US, although since smaller breeds were created, it kinda fell out of favor with families.

Now that's a pity because the Dutch has an adorable personality and is very well-suited to first-time rabbit owners. It's important to remember, however, that this is a very sociable and curious rabbit breed, so it needs toys and lots of playtime to stay happy.

LIONHEAD

The Lionhead rabbit does not only look cute but also hilarious because of their longer than usual fur, especially around their heads.

Yep... they look just like little lions!

This is one of the world's newest rabbit breeds and was only brought to the US, from Belgium, in 1998. They are pretty small and usually weigh about three pounds. Mind you, with their fluffy heads, they are pretty hard to miss despite their small stature. Because of their charming personality and looks, they quickly became popular.

They are very energetic, playful, and curious and make great pets. However, given their long fur, they also need a lot of brushing.

CHECKERED GIANT RABBIT

Weighing in at a whopping **THIR-TEEEEN pounds**, presenting the Checkered Giant Rabbit!

With its spotted fur and humongous size, the Checkered Giant joins the Giant Flemish as one of the largest breeds in the world. In fact, the breed was created over 100 years ago by breeding the Giant Flemish with spotted French lops. So the two giants are closely related indeed.

Now, we would forgive you if you wanted to dive right in and give this one a cuddle, but kids, we urge you to be careful. Given their big size, the Checkered Giant is mostly a pet for grown-ups: they are heavy, big, and can get easily injured if picked up and dropped. They also need a lot of space (both indoor and outdoor). Overall, they are gentle, good-natured, and curious but not nearly as cuddly as many other breeds of domestic rabbits.

Oh, and you can spot a Checkered Giant Rabbit by the butterfly pattern on their (**boop!**) noses.

EUROPEAN RABBIT

The European is the most widespread rabbit species in the world – you might even call this the 'original' domesticated rabbit breed.

You see, all domesticated rabbit species originated from the European Rabbit. This means they all came from this bread at the start, and then ones with different traits were bred specifically to create other sub-breeds.

Yep, the American and Flemish Giant breeds also came from the European!

In rabbit studies, this is known as an Old-World species, meaning it is one of the oldest breeds that originated in Europe and was then exported to just about every corner of the world.

The European is known for digging very complex underground tunnels, with multiple burrows linking to one another and having various entrances and exits. This allows many rabbits, up to around 12 in fact, to live together in the same '*dug out, rabbit city*.'

These underground burrows are called **warrens**, and they can be very wide indeed. So wide that they can cause environmental damage if created in a fragile ecosystem. If European rabbit populations are not kept under control in some regions of the world, the animals are then considered pests.

What is a pest, you ask?

Pests are animals that are introduced to an environment that is not their natural area, and they then go on to cause problems for all other native animals living there. They are not bad animals, to be fair (***because NO animal is bad!***), but if one type is introduced to a new area, it can damage the delicate natural balance in that area. In this case, the animal is considered to be a 'nuisance.' A pest!

INTERESTING FACT: Rabbits are one of only a handful of animals in the world that are considered either pets, breeding stock (for meat and fur), or pests, depending on where in the world you are!

Now that we've learned a little more about the different species and breeds of rabbits found all over the world, it's time to step back in time and find out more about the history of these very special animals.

WHY DID THE BUNNY CROSS THE ROAD?

to prove he could hip hop!

THE HISTORY OF RABBITS

WHERE'D THEY COME FROM?

The fossil trail suggests that the ancestors of rabbits evolved in Asia about 40 million years ago, long before the continents split up and created the ones we know today. This was during a period called **Eocene.**

Scientists believe that when this very old mega-continent split up, rabbits managed to hang on to every broken-up region, and that's how they ended up all over the world.

Now, here's an awesome fact. Did you know that the country Spain was called "The Land of Rabbits" by ancient merchants? *Yep, that's true!*

That's evidence that rabbits were numerous in Europe and, if you remember, it's from these wild rabbits that all other domesticated rabbits originated.

Due to rabbits' fast reproduction, adaptable nature, and because they went to lands where they did not have a lot of predators, their population increased in a lot of different countries all over the world.

FUN FACT: When Rome conquered Spain, the mighty Romans tried to put rabbits in enclosures but the rabbits escaped by digging tunnels.

WHEN DID HUMANS FIRST DOMESTICATE RABBITS?

By now, we know that rabbits existed on earth for millions of years. However, you're probably wondering when humans started to keep them as livestock and pets. Experts agree that wild rabbits were first **domesticated** (this means they were 'trained' to live side by side with humans) over 1,500 years ago. The first people to tame wild rabbits were probably monks living in France!

Almost straight away, monks began breeding different kinds of rabbits to create what we now know as different 'breeds,' which resulted in rabbits of all colors, shapes, and sizes. For many centuries, rabbits were bred and kept much like how people now keep sheep and cows – mostly for their meat and fur.

Only in the last 200 years or so have people all over the world started to keep rabbits as pets, much like cats and dogs. Paintings from 500 years ago actually show rabbits in all sorts of colors and sizes, meaning humans have obviously been very fond of rabbits for a very long time.

ARE RABBITS CLOSELY RELATED TO ANY OTHER ANIMAL?

Yes indeed, rabbits are closely related to rodents. But you might be surprised to know that rabbits are also related to none other than us humans along with primates that include apes and monkeys.

Surprising? *Nature works in mysterious ways, don't you think?*

Rabbits are also close relatives of tree shrews as well as colugos, which are very unique gliding lemurs that live in Asia. *Isn't it interesting to know rabbits have cousins that look so different to them all over the world?*

A tree shrew relaxing on a branch.

WHAT DID THE RABBIT SAY TO THE CARROT?

"It's been nice gnawing you."

WHERE DO RABBITS LIVE?

We now know that rabbits live all over the world, right? In Asia, Europe, the Americas, and Africa, *they really are everywhere!* But is there any place in the world where there are more rabbits, and what kinds of areas do rabbits love to hang out in?

Rabbits are found in almost all land areas of the world. Still, they are noticeably absent in the southernmost part of Southern America, Madagascar, the West Indies, and most of the islands in Southeast Asia. Rabbits are found in many ecosystems such as forests, grasslands, meadows, tundra, wetlands, and even in deserts. That's how adaptable and versatile rabbits are. *Amazing, right?*

At this point, it is important to point out that domesticated rabbits are not nearly as sturdy as wild rabbits. Because they have been bred to live in homes, pet rabbits need a little extra protection – not only from bigger animals but also from things like freezing cold or steaming hot weather. In the wild, rabbits are very good at solving their own problems, but as pets, they depend on humans to keep them healthy and happy.

Hey... do you know how wild rabbits survive in the wilderness?

We bet you know this one!

Rabbits build their own clever homes right into the ground. They dig tunnels and burrows, and that's where they run to whenever there is a threat nearby.

Can you imagine building your own home-sweet-home underground? We think that would be pretty neat!

A tunnel dug by rabbits serves as not only their homes for sleeping but also for nesting, which means this is where mama rabbit hides when she's about to have her babies. From their underground tunnels, rabbits dig many different holes, so they have a lot of escape routes in case of emergencies.

In the wild, rabbits have many predators... and no, we don't just mean humans who hunt them for their fur. Animals like hawks, owls, eagles, wolves, bobcats, and even foxes, all regularly hunt rabbits to eat. It makes a lot of sense, then, to dig an underground safe-haven!

HEY THERE, WHAT'S HOPPIN'?

INTERESTING CHARACTERISTICS AND APPEARANCES OF RABBITS!

Creatures on our planet evolve based on their needs to survive. Evolution may take millions of years to show real change. From that, we know how important certain body parts and functions are to a species for them to not go extinct.

Rabbits are not immune to evolution. They have also developed their bodies for survival, most especially in the wild. So, curious to know which body parts of rabbits they use to live a long and healthy life? We are too!

A rabbit's **teeth, fur, ears, and legs** have special functions, and they rely on these body parts mostly for their day-to-day activities.

Did you know that their **teeth** don't stop growing, ever? Rabbits have two pairs of sharp front teeth or incisors, one at the top and one at the bottom, that they use to gnaw.

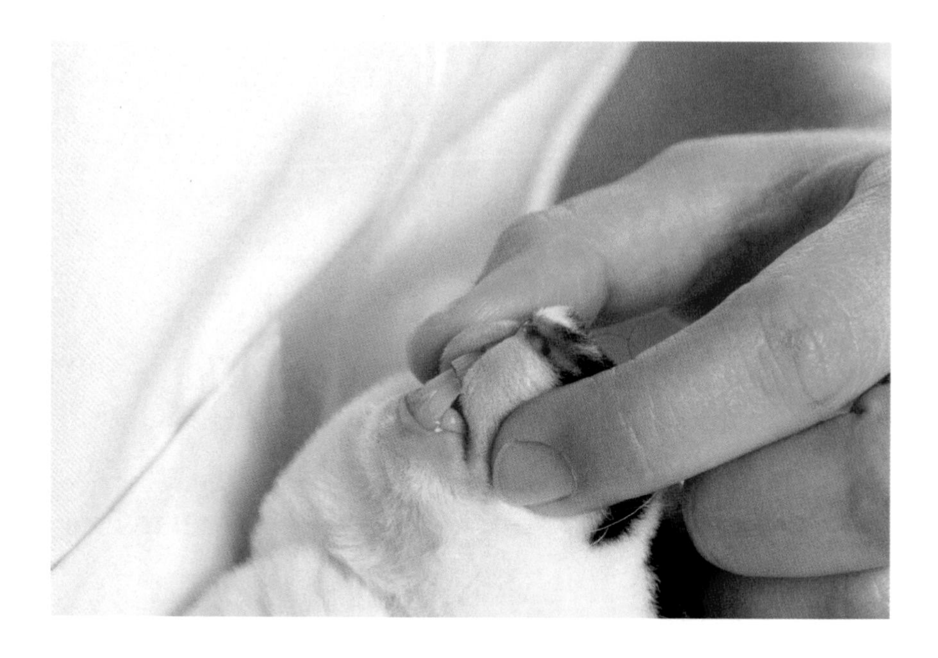

They then have two peg teeth right behind their top incisors. *Do you know of another familiar animal that has teeth that don't stop growing?* We will give you one minute to try and guess (*or look up online*)...

– time's up!

The answer is a horse!

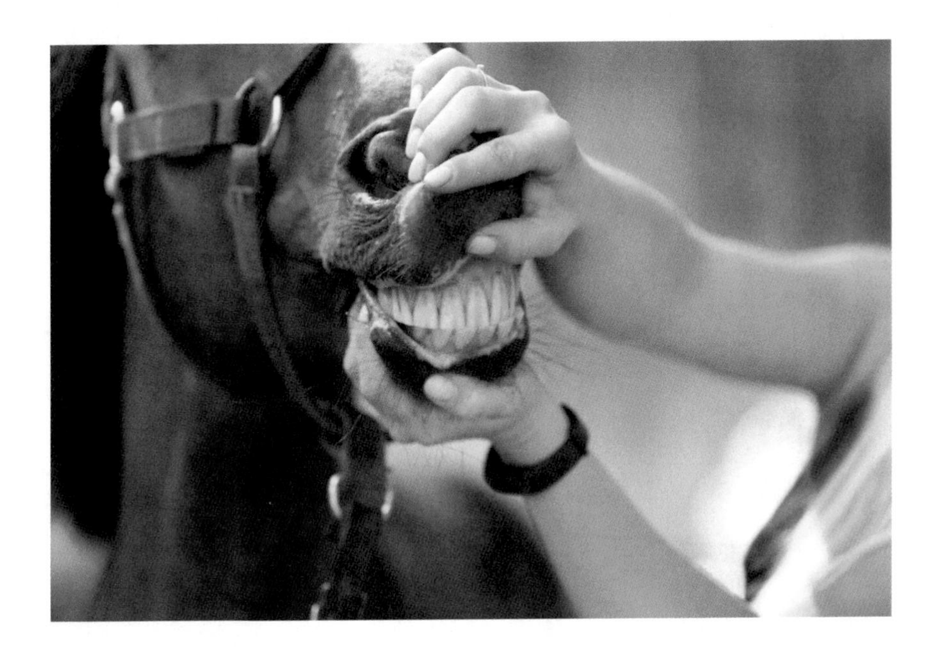

Yes, a horse's teeth also don't stop growing. So, kids, if ever your rabbit's teeth are overgrown, make sure to tell your parents about it so you can take them to the vet for a checkup. It might be hard for them to eat if they are uncomfortable with their overgrown teeth.

Aside from teeth, a rabbit's **fur** is also important as it helps regulate their body temperature. Naturally, the hotter the habitat of a rabbit, the thinner their fur, and the colder the habitat, the thicker the fur!

Now, can you guess which other parts of their bodies help regulate their temperatures? *Oh, this is a tough one to guess...* it's their **ears** of all things!

A rabbit's ears are not just large to make them look cute but are actually pretty useful too. Their ears help in what we call **thermoregulation.** It essentially helps them keep cool when it's hot, and they also help the body release heat when it gets cold. Now that's quite neat!

What's interesting is that rabbits living in hotter climates have larger ears because they need more cooling. That's why rabbits that live in cold countries usually have much smaller ears.

Now let's move on to rabbit **legs and feet**, perhaps the most unique characteristic of this very fascinating animal.

At first glance, rabbits don't look like they would run very fast but, wouldn't you know it, rabbits can run faster than most pet cats! The fastest species of rabbits are the European and Jack, which can sprint at speeds between 25 and 45 miles per hour!

Using their powerful hind legs, rabbits can easily push themselves to either hop or run fast. This also helps rabbits to get away from potential predators. Their hind legs have four toes that are webbed, and they spread as they go for a jump.

THE LIFE CYCLE OF RABBITS

Rabbits, on average, live for about 8 to 10 years.

A young rabbit's life is grouped into five stages:

- Baby – 0 to 3 months of age
- Adolescent – from 3 to 6 months of age
- Teenager – from 6 to 12 months
- Adult – from 1 to 7 years
- Senior – from 7 years onwards

Rabbits have different needs as they grow, which means their food and desire to play, run, and exercise varies depending on their age.

Rabbits are considered seniors once they reach seven years old and above. They may need a lot of care at this stage but take note that rabbits can reach over 10 years old when taken care of properly.

WHY DON'T RABBITS GET HOT IN THE SUMMER?

They have hare conditioning!

A COLLECTION OF FUN FACTS ABOUT RABBITS!

Here are some more super cool facts about rabbits you'll love to know!

- Are you familiar with the rabbit binky? A binky refers to when rabbits are happy and flick their heads and legs. ***It's so adorable!***
- A female rabbit is called a **doe**, like a deer, while a male rabbit is called a **buck.**
- A rabbit's ears can rotate 270 degrees, which means they can turn them all the way back!

- Rabbits may seem well-behaved, but they actually make a lot of noise!

- Another fantastic fact about rabbits is that they can pretty much see all the way around, even to the back of their heads! This is useful in spotting predators from afar so they can make a swift escape.
- Rabbits are very social animals, so be sure to always keep at least two of them so they won't get lonely. You know a rabbit is sad and lonely when it stops being active and crouches in a corner.

HOW DO YOU KNOW CARROTS ARE GOOD FOR YOUR EYES?

Because you never see a bunny wearing glasses!

RABBITS AS PETS

DO RABBITS MAKE GOOD PETS?

Rabbits can make perfect pets indeed, although they do require love and care, as is the case with *every animal* kept as a family pet. Given humans have bred so many different types of rabbits specifically to be kept as pets, you will find many breeds live very happily in a home.

Rabbits are insanely adorable, and the best pet breeds are curious, cuddly, friendly, and good-natured. They can be curious like cats, loyal like dogs, and just as cute as both. Rabbits offer comfort just like other animals that are deemed as pets would. Most are pretty small, so they don't take up much space at all.

However, and no matter how **BIG** or *small*, all rabbits need plenty of space, safety, exercise, a healthy rabbit diet, and a lot of love. When considering getting ***any*** animal as a pet, it's important to remember that your pet will very much depend on you for its very survival.

TIPS FOR HOW TO TAKE CARE OF RABBITS? (BONUS SECTION!)

Are you interested in finding out how to take good care of rabbits as pets?

We've got you!

Here are some tips you might find helpful:

FOOD!

Rabbits are **herbivores** which means that they eat plants. They eat mostly grass and leaves but also flowers and fruits. Make sure that they eat their share of grass hay because that's very important to their diet and health.

They also need their fair share of green foods. Some of their favorites are kale, broccoli, romaine lettuce, dandelion greens, brussel sprouts, parsley, and celery.

Feed them a good balance of fruits and vegetables, and they'll be good to go!

Did you know rabbits can easily get fat? Although you can buy commercial pellets for rabbits, this rich food should not be a regular part of their diet.

A very curious aspect of rabbits is that they cannot vomit when they eat something icky. At first, this might seem like a good thing, right? Because who likes to clean up vomit?! Yet, in reality, this makes rabbits very delicate when it comes to what they eat. This is why it is so important to feed pet rabbits **ONLY** food that is good and healthy for them to eat. Because they cannot vomit when they eat the wrong food, they can get very sick very quickly if they ever do.

OVERALL HEALTH!

The first thing you should always do when you get a pet rabbit is to take it to the vet so an expert can tell you exactly what your rabbit should be eating and how much!

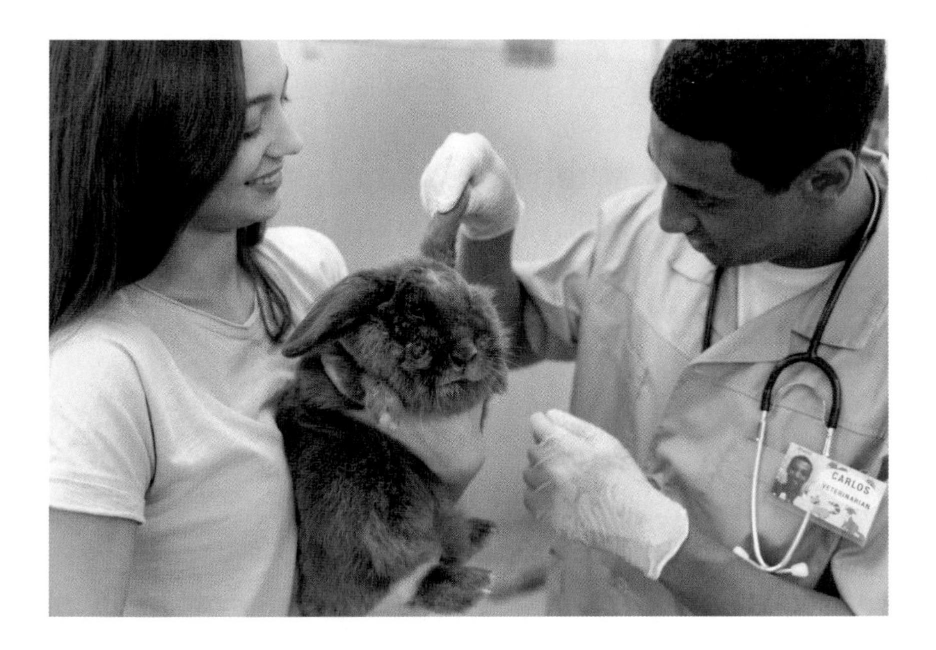

- Make sure that water is always available for them. This is very important!
- Make sure that their living area is well-ventilated and has enough room for exercise.
- Don't forget that rabbits need some form of hiding or resting area.
- Always handle your rabbit very gently, they may look sturdy, but rabbits are, in fact, very fragile animals.

NEUTERING

Neutering your rabbits is a very good option to consider. Wondering what neutering is? In case you didn't know, neutering means removing the reproductive organ of your beloved pet so they cannot have babies. It might sound a bit harsh, but it actually is good for them in the long run, especially if you plan to have more than one rabbit! Not only will this ensure you don't end up with hundreds of rabbits in a few years (*oops!*), but it can also stop them from becoming aggressive. All in all, considering rabbits can quickly become pests in the wrong circumstances, it is a good idea to have your pet rabbit neutered when it is about 6 months of age. And don't worry, your vet will guide you (*and your rabbit!*) through the procedure.

Good stuff to know, right?

These are our top tips for you to ensure that your rabbit lives a happy and healthy life!

THERE'S JUST NO BUNNY LIKE YOU!

THANK YOU FOR READING

Rabbits are one of the most iconic creatures ever, and we sure enjoyed sharing fun and valuable things about them with you! We hope that you enjoyed our little journey with them as much as we did.

On behalf of all the rabbits of the world, we say a heartfelt **THANK YOU** for loving them so much!

But your rabbit journey need not end here!

Why not share all you learned with your friends and family so they too can know all about the exciting things we learned about bunny rabbits!

If you've enjoyed this book, please let us know by leaving a rating and a brief review wherever you made your purchase! This helps us spread the word to other readers! Thank you for your time, and have an awesome day!

For more information, and to find more great reads about awesome animals please visit:

www.animalreads.com/books/

We look forward to sharing the next journey with you as we get to know all the amazing creatures with whom we share our world!

HAVE A FLUFFY DAY!

ISBN: 978-3-96772-081-5

ISBN: 978-3-96772-082-2

Animal Reads at www.animalreads.com

Published by Admore Publishing: Roßbachstraße, Berlin, Germany

www.admorepublishing.com

REFERENCES

Interested in learning more about rabbits?

Check out some of these great resources online. Some of the information on these pages were even used to help create this book.

- https://www.livescience.com/28162-rabbits.html
- https://www.wonderopolis.org/wonder/what-is-the-difference-between-a-rabbit-and-a-hare
- https://wagwalking.com/breed/top-most-popular-rabbit-breeds
- https://www.goodhousekeeping.com/life/pets/g26950009/best-rabbit-breeds/

- https://www.amnh.org/research/science-news/2006/earliest-rabbit-fossil-found-suggests-modern-mammal-group-emerged-as-dinosaurs-faced-extinction
- https://www.livescience.com/28162-rabbits.html
- https://www.vetcarepethospital.ca/beginners-guide-to-pet-rabbit-care/
- https://www.oxbowanimalhealth.com/blog/rabbit-life-stages/
- https://www.columbushumane.org/the-wag/2019/2/20/fun-facts-about-rabbits

Made in the USA
Monee, IL
04 July 2022

cad81055-e84e-4807-9f74-bea05ad069b9R01